We Travel Towards It

We Travel Towards It

Amy Pence

SERVING
HOUSE
BOOKS

We Travel Towards It

Copyright © 2025 Amy Pence
First Edition

Paperback ISBN: 9781947175723

Library of Congress Control Number: 2025935922

All rights reserved. No part of this book may be reproduced or transmitted in any form or by any means, electronic, digital, or mechanical, including photocopy, audio recording, or any information storage and retrieval system, without prior permission from the publisher or author (except by reviewers who may quote brief passages).

Cover art "Crown" by Dorothy O'Connor
Author photo by Ada Montgomery

Exterior design by Jacob Arms
Published by Serving House Books
Lawrence Landing Company
Raleigh, North Carolina 27609
USA, North America

Serving House Books is a proud member of:

Independent Book Publishers Association
 and
Community of Literary Magazines and Presses

www.servinghousebooks.com

SERVING HOUSE BOOKS

ADVANCE PRAISE

Beginning from "the instant...the oak fell," destroying the poet-speaker's house on top of her, *We Travel Towards It* embarks on an awakening born of ruin at once personal and collective—the tree's fall a consequence of climate change-intensified storms. Pence digs into memory, uprooting personal as well as societal traumas of gendered and environmental violence born of desire's "endless pursuit, grasping at what / was never ours." In these unsettling, empowering poems, Pence insists on the necessity of remembering not only "inviolable wonder" but "what is frail / what is brutal / what pearls under the feet." Truth-seeking and transformative, the poems of *We Travel Towards It* are as gorgeous as they are devastating.

    —Sandra Meek, Author of *Still* and *Ecology of Elsewhere*

In the aftermath of personal disaster—a storm-felled tree that cleaved a house and a life in two—Amy Pence writes, "It was good to fill the sinkhole myself." Both metaphor and fact, the "storied canopies" of the fallen tree and the gap left in its place provide an opening to probe past losses, beauties, and griefs. *We Travel Towards It* moves deftly between the personal and the public, from the cleaving of childbirth to the anonymous intimacies of strangers sharing hotels after the ever-intensifying natural disasters on the planet we all call home. Surprising and urgent in the face of climate catastrophe, this is a remarkable collection.

    —Chelsea Rathburn, Author of *Still Life with Mother and Knife*
        and Poet Laureate of Georgia

For Ada . hummingbird

Contents

{-}

Red Oak, Black Oak	1
The Dash	2
Communion	3
Unsalvageable + Scented	4
Sour-Sweet	5
Uprooted	6
Disaster Relief	7
The Trans-Apocalypse	8

{-}

Annihilation	11
Lives of the Great Composers	12
The Ledgers	13
Bayou Ghost Trees	14
Death-Moth	15
Manhattan	16
The Place Where You Were Killed	17

{-}

Those Ghost Selves	21
Footnoting Luce	22
Baby Teeth	23
Jekyll	24
Cabinet of Obsessions	25
The Omitted Center	27

{-}

Fireflied	31
Enter at Castello di Vezio	32
Calaveras Big Trees	33
The Movable Charolais	34

Hover	35
Birthday Month	36
The Death Verses	37
Monet at Palazzo Contarini	38

{-}

O My Visitor: A Travelogue	41

{-}

One, Another	49
Snake Notice	50
Honeymoon	51
A Sonic Crown of Bees	52
Grammar	53

{-}

The Fantasists of the Earth	57
Mourning Dove	58
Jewelweed	60
Creaturely	61
Ghost Pipes	62
Dendrochronology	64
Trees Flee	65

{-}

Notes

Acknowledgments

...when I lean over the chasm of myself—
it seems
my god is dark
and like a web: a hundred roots
silently drinking.

This is the ferment I grow out of.

More I don't know, because my branches
rest in deep silence, stirred only by the wind.

Rainer Maria Rilke

Red Oak, Black Oak

Fog-locked trees
bear   forward
mute   insular
        close
unclothed
  not   dis
closing
bound by root
   subterraneous
leaf - shorn
   time waved
rocky insomniacs
marching
ghost -   like
    back-lit
         sketched
  our
         branches
arterial
       pumping
dormant   seeds
we   gather   gray
frayed   by winter
sentient   red oak
burr oak   black
our mantras   like egos
resolving   dis
integrating
         silvered
on   the horizon
ancestors   conjoin

three   generations
          in the photo
I pass
by   them
each   morning
arranging   my
self   for the day
each   dead
faces   the flash
two wear   fifties
pillbox   hats
my   grandmothers
iron board   flat
my mother   beams
holds a fragment : me
my sister   grasps
father's hand
just she and I   now
left alive   all their
grievances   adventures
mis   takes
extinguished by this day
my uncle our only suicide
still   a crewcut boy
wears a look   acute
with longing   forms
incarnate   &   crumble
as Grandmother did   when
she found him   stilled
amid smoke   lo, we
abide close &   a part

The Dash

– to run or travel in great hurry . Of the instant .   the oak fell - splintered & splintering . Of the instinct, our primeval falling . to hold to what's already found . *- to strike with violence so as to break into fragments* . Of wet ground, its feral mouth . bursting full born into storm . Of that thread between – taut & troubled,   the elemental rosebud when she came glistening from my body . hair almost inhuman . Of thought's needles, prime . puncturing . *- to destroy, ruin, confound* . Of time :   clock face, rock face . slum in my mansion . wind in my stillness . the delicate eons of a second . they call it *samadhi* . a deepening absorbing surprise . as in *this could be my last thought* . as in *this is what happens when you die* . Of this romance, life . this yes . that *that*. *- to put down on paper, throw off, or sketch* .   whole in my brokenness . All in my Missingness . a path to what will happen . before it even occurs . Of what binds us, the umbilical . Of the carnal, its arching. catapult to a dry version of this flesh . *- to bring to nothing, to spoil* . Thread entering the lips, suturing the secrets . stitching the unspoken . what we were told had never occurred . *- to draw through so as to erase* .   the em dash— not the en-dash . Of the tempest, my mother, & formlessness . Of my loss as I ran to the door .   *- used as a euphemism for damn* .   Of this quick inevitable slice .   my core : yours

Communion

You know . that winter . after the fall of our displacement . after Harvey . Irma . after Maria . water glutting the streets . we were stacked in a suites hotel with adjusters and contractors from out of state . entire families with dogs . a few of us - alone . we passed each other in the hall . carpet dank from boots scuffing up stairs . that fall I knelt on the bathmat . cried each day for 37 days .   in that mid-grade impersonal hotel . you know . that winter of mudslides . after the fires of Napa Valley . after the shootings at a concert in Las Vegas .   arms were thrown over the ones they loved . arms thrown . in the evenings men gathered at the tarped pool with beers . contrails etched a weakening sky . they sat on plastic chairs playing guitars. sometimes a uke . sometimes that humming fool, the harmonica .   I opened the window to hear that sound . Looked down on their heads bent in a rough circle . some balding . some with ragged ponytails . grief for what we lost . what we're losing .   let's say we are shipwrecked .   let's say we are fools . climate change, inertia .   we pass each other in the halls . avert our eyes .

because we are exposed .   because we didn't see it coming

Unsalvageable + Scented

Blue wax cubes
leftover, it appears
from a previous life.

Before the disaster,
three shootings, a contagion—
before the dream

life. Housed in plastic
as everything houses
in plastic: sandwiches

tampons, me
in a cubicle. 3-D printers
shitting out all

the facsimiles. Cubes
a *mix of musk,*
cedar, a touch of

mystery. I'm
reminded of a man
overwrought

with cologne. I'm reminded
of humankind. Who
said we were kind?

Reality has the audacity
to be breakable. Looks
like I melted one

cube of Illusion
before my house
came down. Reeks

like nothing broken
into shapes of
nothing. One

doorknob's turn
from death—huffing
on wonder.

Sour-Sweet

I enter the museum of grief . carrying my notebook . a small blued body once drowned . I pick up my daughter's toys as if moving through wax . but she is grown now and gone . I enter the essay . follow my student down the streets of old Kabul . stand as he raps his young man knuckles on the plain wooden door looking for Afsana . Remember her dark eyes . the jaguar pendant she wore ? they ate ice cream together from a stall . sour, then sweet one dusty July . before the troops moved in . the museum is made of human tissue . Paki a grown man stands 5 feet 4 inches tall . his first memory :   Buduburam the refugee camp in Ghana . I'm on the back of his uncle's motor scooter   before the accident . his cousin balanced like complicated fruit on handlebars . hunger a temple we carry everywhere . roadside a ghost or maybe a witch wears his dead aunt's face . afterwards only Paki walks away alive . there are places we'll never enter again . relics scattered in the crushed house : oranged in light's flapping tarp . another woman writes of rape by her father . *it's only a story* she says . but our eyes turn to milk under the fluorescent lights . in the museum we shovel our errors . pillars torn down . artifacts raided . when we sit close enough .   loss's beads collect around us :   azurite . the jaguar's head .
        deep garnet .   wrinkle   .   with the resilience of hands

Uprooted

It was good to fill the sinkhole myself. After the landscaper
botched the job. Beneath the plant he poised, thirsty
on red clay: divots of emptiness. Ten bags of top soil
go in smelling of the deciduous northern states, released
from tight plastic bags, hugging dirt like a girdle.
I want to throw in my worn underwear,
mover's boxes, insurance adjusters wearing
snide smiles. I want to throw in the site
of trauma, but here it is as I tap the spade down – the gap
the massive oak left and how it will open
every year, unhinging its jaws.
I used to listen to the tree's elocutions: its deep
drinking, its network of mouths—
felt the mastery of its anomalous hide.
I heard its power, wind in its canopy indigent. Then
the scavenger dawns, my rapacious need
for touch, pretending
I liked it, saying *really it's okay*,
when he pulled out. But it wasn't.
The way he turned me face-down in the middle
of the night, used his wrestler's move:
his left knee on the back of my left knee, pinning
me until he was satisfied. It was
a happen. A thing. A toy
called nothingness. *You can't
always get what you want.* I dream the familiars
signaling underground to let the tree go.
The new oaks and the ancients. All that
subterraneous asking, and the polite refusals.
Weakened by hurricane, weakened
by every sonic storm, the rape of the last century,
the rape of this one. Released finally—
the earth opening, then the thudding fall.

Disaster Relief

Without you, my dreams have coarsened, become
less prophetic. Indifferent even. As
you, that last morning in the bad hotel, boxy
neon wall tags signaling what was inevitable.
A morning's dull commute under arching
trees—driving into what I mistake for
a sunrise apricoting the sky, then
the intersection. Cars aflame, folding
into the dung beetles of the apocalypse.
Commentary from the dream watcher: *Remember
the fires we created? Unnatural and
racing to their source? You came to my aid once,
the two of us flaring—powers transforming*. Then
the planet's roll and shift into cinders.

The Trans-Apocalypse[1]

That which we do not bring into consciousness

appears in our lives as fate. Jung's words

stoke their carnal embers and you remember

several junctures when you could have been compliant,

but broke your life into sticks. In the dream,

it was always far in the future: an earthquake,

nuclear winter—ash upon ash. Could you

have predicted the present— a slow burn splayed across

brown hills or the penetrating hurricane—growing wetter

over heated waters—to take your house down? You are in it:

the body toxic and fingered with use.

Do you see the bleak harmony

of stars? If they were written

for you, they obscure.

---

[1] the phase climate futurists say we now live in:
a reality in which humans engage constantly with ecological threats

Annihilation

Fathers die & mothers . sometimes before they are ready . usually before we are . your mother at 85 . my father at 58 . sometimes dark matter tumbles down sky-worn imitating clouds . the stitchery where trees once were . graves open to release the owls we have forgotten . train cars pitch forward . carry human faces blank & blinking . overhead planes hold humans upright in seats as we spool through the past . homebound to Hartsfield an image floats piecemeal from the mind bin : how my father holds himself still . unsure what my boyfriend did . or why I called him . bruises gather at my neck . plush as   roses . a palimpsest . a grim joke : a choker . my boyfriend held me down so long stars exploded in the dark universe of mind .   on the back-stoop I can't invite my father in his eyes saturate with blue .

      didn't I dream my father years after he died ?

Flat out on a field of grass next to the train tracks . trains doppler past our bodies . mouths open to laugh in a pulsing rain . we laughed so hard we merged .   trains float & pitch   over every inviolable wonder :   we travel towards it

Lives of the Great Composers

Snow falls over the grave of Vivaldi .   a simple grave in Vienna .   over the grave of Bach that lover of the fugue .   unmarked for over 150 years .   snow falls on the grave of Thelonious Monk in Englewood, New Jersey .   seeds like sprockets from cottonwood trees. float through the window   . past the veteran reading a war poem .   clusters float . pell mell . slo mo .   go with that clot in the throat .   seeds fall .   snow . unremarkable . carries its own soft symphony .   falls into earth's creases   . *The Lives of the Great Composers* . a forgotten book .   unknown even now to my stepfather   .   who gave it to me years ago .   it frustrated me then   . as if—why would I want such a book ?   now his brain washes away . ischemia— the deep white matter . subcortical lacunes : clinically silent .   when it snowed that rare snow in Las Vegas my stepfather slept . or played piano on the Strip . hunched over like Thelonius Monk . wasn't I afraid of that Jekyll & Hyde ? when he rose from the piano—whom might he be ? snow of a slow-growing dementia .   falls through the brain . snow falls as if we won't remember : over four thousand dead .   not including the injured . we let go .   try to forget .   minds fill with snow .   or with a heat so suffocating bodies collapse around them .   the poem stops falling in the room .   goes on re-seeding . the forgetful stand in the snow   & those we forget suffer   their exposure .   because we do not want them .   do not want the themes of history :   the preponderance, the fugue .   *before you know it*, my stepfather says . looking at the forgotten . *they're all grown up* .   his face uncomposed .   before you know it . you will lie on the ground with your mouth open . ice collects in the joints .   numbness pools at the back of your head .
  Thelonius Monk plays his discordant chords

The Ledgers

--for Valerie, on the death of her father Ramón Martinez

We collect the names of the dead . we recollect the names of the dead . the mind is a page . the mind shifts its wings . letters etched on paper . paper carried by many beaks . the mind – fluted - is Borromini's staircase : its marble infinity all we can imagine of the dead . your father sang happy birthday in his native Spanish . sang in the grand courtyard at the Hotel Santa Fe . in the ledgers of the dead - names disarrange their wings - turn their large heads . your father gone & mine . names that never met . awake my last night in Rome - I have taken all the photographs . hear weighted calls of a hundred geese drifting past . three a.m. - headed where - I cannot say . when he walked the sidewalks of Hartford to work - you could set your watch by Wallace Stevens . the rational mind floated above him . evenings : *the palm at the end of the mind* . I open black shutters - lean into the mouth of Rome . watch formations - obscuring . *Selah, tempestuous bird* . your father sang happy birthday. we were forty then . your father taught Math - made sure every fork nestled one way . in his attic Wallace Stevens exacted each word . *like excellence collecting excellence* . while his wife suffered his absence . some days your father could not rise from his bed . Ramón, Ramón – in your clear baritone : Borromini's staircase . I hear the names of the dead shouted across Rome . hear them echoing . light forges a pattern in gold - a ladder with its helix in names . Ramón, I am sleepless

Bayou Ghost Trees

Rough planks over the swamps at Barataria
        century-old bald cypresses rise
                brackish the water—
the day crafty with scent
    Jean Lafitte waits—*by all accounts*
        a handsome man, calls himself a privateer
                never say pirate to his face
Wet leaves mulch— insects work soil
        turn every flesh effigy into sand
                Barataria : all the lakes, swamps & bays south
                    of New Orleans—Gulf of Mexico, Grand Isle, Grande Terre
Light apricots over bayou's pseudo-acacia
        suspending her seed pods—
            pirates infiltrate the *myriad bayous*
                all the way to New Orleans--impossible to patrol
Was there a tear in the portal? Were you—
        Stepfather—quite near? *By 2050, with no intervention,*
            Grand Terre will disappear
At dusk, creatures arrive
        a gator shifts, night shrouds its body
            the birthplace of the Lafittes: could be Port-au-Prince,
                San Domingo or Bayonne, France
My stepfather looked out a window, dying
        leaves lapped backward in the small red maple
            some majestic sleep: as in some tether—
                hurricane winds favored bald cypress, water tupelo, button bush
                a tear in the universe—
What forms will it take?
        the bodies, after the hurricane, putrefy—
            sink, then rise
                Over the swamp's muddy listen
                    seed pods suspend : withered
                        multiple forms attach to source
Legends of Lafitte flourish: King Arthur or Robin Hood? smuggling contraband, luxuries
        Sway the leaves, dear father : saturate this landscape
            seeds in-dwell— hold being's many
                forms : atoms, the void—
Weather : marauder   .   whether to be human

Death-Moth

Often on the drive home . 400 to 285 . gadding the flat magnanimous I-20 . I almost see you . your high collar . profile, seedy . you—my Keats—incarnate . beside these papers I'll grade by Tuesday . your eyes unmoored by poverty .   eyes oceanic in a face .   fated   with waiting or the future . the one I drive into—   keen and fitful amnesia bin   . if I were to call to you from the 21st century   . would you   . on a tubercular evening . punctuated by parlor drama & coughing . could you .   in your dying . slipping as we do   . cell from cell— fathom me ?   all the deans are dead now . even then, Dr. Nan grading my nod to *Endymion* . carried a cancer . her eyes pained . silently as she marked . in Rome, I found your life-mask . then, your death-mask .   looked up   to painted finials that plundered you on the ceiling . amid the bloodletting . amid your cries . to be loosened from *this posthumous life* . I drive full into the highway's gloaming . papers at my side . that I will mark .   though now they shudder . because *Thou Shalt Remain, in Midst of Other Woe* .   *Don't apologize,* Dr. Nan said, *for what you know.* are we not an age's consciousness *unravished* ? minus the *timbrels*— minus even my *melancholy* . now suppressed .   are we not all posthumous ? living our deaths . intimates of time .   one page rises to bat at the window. a *death-moth—* . You—my Keats—gaze sky-ward .   exhaust the centuries   .   like fuel

Manhattan

Chimney - my mother says from dream-life - *ashes* . my skull's shaved .   exfoliated by experts . next in line to be nude before a clatter of former models . I might be the old one . or the small one . or the plump one .   *armor* my mother says .   *mettle* .   I wear only my red leather boots . ones crafted to take me back through the subways of Manhattan . 1981 . perhaps this was before you were even conceived . can you conceive . the *you* reading this . that   I was walking Park Avenue when I passed Jackie O . then Martin Mull ? days later Madeline Kahn and I sat in the same audience watching *Diner* . but I've eaten all the marzipan roses . in Greenwich Village we laughed at the cock lollipops . I licked every sweetness from my lips . *enjoy it while it lasts*   my mother says .   *too bad about your short legs* .   my skull stipples with new growth . gone white as chicken feathers . I see them approaching from the lakebed . teenage girls . finally freed from their rapists . walk toward you .   think about it : most emotions are merely concepts .   the brain . they say. registers only *pleasant unpleasant pain* and *arousal* . everything else is just me penetrating you . or you penetrating me .   I run up the subway steps in 1981 . before you even occurred . the assault not what I expected . *your hair has always been lanky* . my mother says .   *what happened to your chin?* I'm wearing my red boots . I'm wearing sirens .   I'm wearing Emily Dickinson's copper hair . splotches hit the steps and trail me on West 56th .   all the way to the apartment .   *ashes* . my mother says .   *I'm just ashes* .   I   waken .   arms thrown back .

The Place Where You Were Killed

The pin oak comes down
knees crumbling
a spider retreats, its web torn by a hand
not unlike Kant's *Ding an sich*
In a glade of ferns
Why were you crying that day you set out
weeping?
the child breaks gradually into   a self
the next
forms elude me
a being
its knees holding the reticence of
Near the tree's hollow
I cannot see   Where you walked,
let's say you were a primitive
I give up the glade of ferns
the woods of your hands in the dog's fur,
When there's just the finest crust
One being followed
When the gun shot sounds
Missing
is like missing Being

Those Ghost Selves

My New Orleans rises from its jewel-box .
urine-soaked alleyways . oil slicks
floating on the Gulf .

scent trails from Market watermelon
split open . winos on street corners
taking my penny or two .

I steer my sister's stroller . dolls
loaded like vienna sausages .
down Decatur Street

into antique shops . their eyes
gelid as fish . Bridget's pressed-in
& looking north .

apartment jammed with sisters .
an infant brother . stepfather & a mother
rejecting all the typical motions

grim nights when we dozed above Bourbon Street .
spattered beer smell rising . jazz
static on speakers . the erotic

disclosing . a stuffed
polar bear kissing
my nine-year-old nipples . rats

rattle under overturned
coffee cans .
this antiquated New

Orleans has aqueous dreams .
eyelashed & closing . oysters
locked, sway under gulf water .

everything rises, disappearing
estuaries erode in silence, blink back
my knock & shame

Footnoting Luce

Irigaray's angel = mobility, multiplicity.
The cleft[1] in the birch's otherworldliness.
When I settle in, all the bees
release their sore honey.
I am fungible[2] - kneel near
the several chanterelles, frilled
for their accelerating de-
composition. Like *sets of lips*
a stacked anonymity.

Ibid the ibid. A dragonfly hovers its
simulacrum[3] - enters the fungi –
thrilling to thrust us
the ibid, op cit, to auto-
erotically, see the all of us.

---

[1] Woman "touches herself" all the time…for her genitals are formed of two lips in continuous contact. Thus, within herself, she is already two—but not divisible into one(s) that caress each other—Luce Irigaray
[2] The society we know, our own culture, is based upon the exchange of women.-LI
[3] So many representations, so many appearances separate us from each other. – LI

Baby Teeth

Among pulled buttons . they are missing .   among thronged sewing needles. not one .   I look in the ebony jewelry box for hazards of my grown girl's growth . find brown-stained . broken-rooted .   a capsized sculptural few .   some like misshapen pearls .   slobbering ache . tormenting when they came in . hardy & hinged abruptions .   before the twisting the pulling   . my dream self wanders through a junkyard . passes all the cars my parents drove . find the finned Cadillac we rode cross-country . my parents blurring highways .   exchange vicious words . when we park near a ground-down cemetery . smell of baloney . the fragmentary dead . do I miss her teething ? . *yes* . stalled in the dream-car with no seatbelt I find my old Barbie case : hollow place where I tuck her outfits . a cavity for those fitful shoes .   that's when my teeth fall out .   soft as chalk . who I had been vanishing . who I could be . a furl . do I miss carrying her upright for hours? . *yes* . sleeplessness exacts the tender . driven to my sorest whorl . air zeroes. wings hover . retrieved from under her warm pillow baby teeth like found coral . in the path of my grown girl . toothy tombstones now .   is it all about endings ? what happened . happened long ago   .   what will happen— has already occurred

Jekyll

The robber barons on Jekyll Island gather . for the first transatlantic call . fluff & puff of their faces . J.P. Morgan . Rockefeller . president of AT&T . all in attendance .   at the center of their inevitable era   . ocean curls over our bodies   . like lace . am I spellbound   -   am I waiting ? President Woodrow Wilson merely listened in . we take the ghost tour trolley to the old cemetery   . in the gap . bardo space . maybe some other estuary .   three ghosts   scatter .   as woodstorks rise from a salt marsh . or wild deer find the shade . was I spellbound ?   did I say like lace ?   was it this existence ? the buried DuBignon . one of the last known slave traders . 1858: I read on the exhibit wall *they stacked 409 Africans like spoons in a yacht repurposed and named* The Wanderer . 79 died . Henri Dubignon profited and never paid . Spanish moss on the live oaks dangle   . did I say Rockefeller ?   did I say we were the ghosts ? . driftwood trees whole and standing . tangled at the root .   history, death, stain of exploitation .   clinging to life   :   what we can never undo   .   the animate net sends crabs   .   running across the hillside .   at our slightest step

Cabinet of Obsessions

    for John Lebo

Rain pummels the garden
a bird decomposes into a small house
heaved up by insects, then breaking apart
entrances   /exits

.

my daughter's seventeen-year-old wings
clipped and stowed in a rough box beneath my bed

.

leaving, her car tires spurn the gravel
a ribcage fills with tiny mites: *ornithonyssus sylviarum*
my ankles break or
her car spins from the road

.

no, the spirit does not enter here

.

watch how art obsesses
Artemisia Gentileschi's sly allegory in self-portraits
paints herself as Judith, hacking at Holofernes' head
looking like Tassi—the one who raped her

.

a fugue of black-whiskered faces
eyes stunned to see the knife

.

my friend John remembers the pompadours
of his James Dean youth
wanted a duck tail like that, lusted
for a girlfriend like that
hiking up on a washing machine
in her short dungarees, how

he wanted to stroke her hair back
between long thin fingers

.

let's catalog these expressions disappearing:
pompadour, dungarees

.
what is frail
what is brutal
what pearls under the feet?
.
Gentileschi peers into the chiaroscuro
Tassi's dismembered head big as a cabbage
.
a longing is not an obsession
I dreamed the slender wings
of what's left of my girl's youth
.
taillights stretch down the driveway
arching pulmonary trees
a morning polished by rain

The Omitted Center

Around which . all the hands in your body go . moths put their tiny labile mouths—night's fret . more intricate than one had supposed . Remember the tantrums, the soiled pants?—there was a time . when the girl lay prone like balsa wood . would not let you go— . Around which .

traffic feeds from the city center.
catacombs spiral.   bridge
darkening the hot   cemented
Around which . the river lesions
hills :   what is shorn was shorn
Fingers pried away from yours :
potential for *yes* .Her sobs slant.
want-want .   Her ragged eyes
her leaving. trepidation as truth.
she had a sister .Her mouth now
know, could you . when she was
stuck wet to her   round and
each defilement ? Around which
done to :   *can I have a sister ?*
from the bed . that one .   that
it's late Miss Dickinson.   her
years later . The Rock of Cashel
the cast-out bodies .   arched
. a hologram for Kings . Around
20 to 285 . succubus   funnel
manicured nails take your   oily
. a school bus hovers close . you
staring out the window .   the
there you were   unverbed .

then away   .   miles and miles —
to concrete & guardrails . oil spots
length speckled to the arduous *no* .
the silent city . Past the moss-crudded
from us :   long and ago   .   Say GO .
don't and *don't* . as if every *no* had the
exclude all possibility but what?   *the*
dim . duskier because court-ordered .
Back from a visitation . said she wished
grown sulky as a teenager :   did you
born .   hot animal with her black hair
fascinating skull . of each defilement—
the ghost sister walked . the one it was
she said . then she'd be the one   drug
other . sometimes . a rap . at the door .
father said . Around which you walked
Ireland—gothic chapel arched around .
around the past's   green & mossed city
which   . traffic vomits its way down
to 400's toll booth .   the platinum
nickels . grimy turn down the turnpike
remember seeing her   . sitting alone .
ghost sister beside her . Because idling
blank-to-blank .   *numb circuit*   .

You could not change what . he did to her . Could not skirt   . the multiverse . an alternate verse . Taking off into night traffic . where you would both turn to ghost . her wan smile . Return to Eternal Return . Back to the city's indigent freeways . her ferocious *no, stop, please* . could you? would you have gone -   left everything to save her?   heads shorn, hair dyed . in disguise .   Exiting the city, leaving— .   light bars   travel across her face's alternate sister .   *numb circuit* .   it's what you didn't do . that you cannot undo

Fireflied

If for 500 lives
I shall be reborn
a fox, then maybe
I've stuck it
to causation.

I held still enough
to hear the deer
unspeckled
with grief.

I was lost enough
to un-find you.
That one martini
was not my undoing,

it was later—we
walked among fireflies
carrying our Dairy
Queens when I knew

I would never inhabit
you again.

Enter at Castello di Vezio

We hike twenty minutes up the hillside of Varenna to Vezio. On the cobblestone path,
two sisters lean together, laugh. Bowers of roses overhang what I cannot grasp—
time's hot scented rosemary. Over the next ridge, olive groves ripple down to what is indigo in
Lago di Como. A hush when we enter the falconry—as if these forms will pass
for the immortal, will turn their tufted heads. A red-tailed hawk, a falcon, the great horned owl
named Artú. In the pools where our eyes meet: prey, predator, a quiet so interior they remain
just fleet & temporary housing for what I may know—when
I cease to know.

Calaveras Big Trees

In my 15th incarnation
I cut and reassembled a sequoia
for the traveling exhibition
in 1860, year of our Lord.

We paraded that giant across
20 states, jigging it together
into spectacle: I did not mourn
the hunted. All
was quiet to myself.

Near death, astral flash of mother
bent near me with tin cup,
my own blind heels
riveting the stump
of the mammoth tree
with 22 other dancers.

Then a shudder through
my blood: two rivers join
the Self to the giant
I murdered.

Root-stomping, we lift
out of time.

The Movable Charolais

White hides in the near evening.
The sensitives stand close.
Big-boned, the oak knuckles up.

Among the herd, speechless
gnostics, sour mosquitoes,
two jackasses tufted
like upholstery. Lowing and the lowly—
what the cows are, lo
I am. What the low call *owl*
gibbers sound from the trees
when the full dark comes on.

Hover

the skin of me has no name . nor the arching branches . against a monochrome forest . nor frogs brimming to the surface . with a million tones . skin on water collects water skaters . skaters on water . lobed leaves & toothed . or unlobed untoothed . less familiar . than the skin of me . on the news images of small dwellings . reports grown men entered girls found hoveled . {related to hove or hover} . in bent refrigerator boxes under half-burnt underpass . {to arch, bend, buckle} . under construction shards . forcibly, they enter the girls . one—11— flesh strafed . burned by a plastic lighter— . men toothed, untoothed . entrances . spaces . invasions . most dark-haired girls . their hair clotted with semen . or secreted in a van . fingers hover : hair covered uncovered . pixels reflect across faces . an eye witnesses a volley {vulgar latin: *volta*, feminine noun} of creatures . creatures volley {to fly, see *volant*} . into the I . interlocking millions . frogs with their bilious croaking . as in *want* . *want* . *want* . matter . body .envelops . {envolupen, to be involved in sin, crime} . girls nameless . entered . entered again . dry leaves . spent shells . skate across water . our skin has no name . nor the interlocking branches . with a million tones . the I speaks blooms . the I wreaks {Olde English: to avenge}.   heaves {past tense, hove; to lift, raise, bear up}   its millions

Birthday Month

You dive-bomb the candle.
The flame sounds, scorching your wings.
        You were my antelope.
        You were my blue heron.
Once I watched
the small pads of your feet
crust with dirt, followed you up
creek. Once I wound down
into Sabino Canyon alone
then waited for your rattles
to cease, rigid as you drew
your organed length away.

Often, August, I hear your eerie
calls from overlarge tulip trees
though I cannot spy the bird
where you reside. Leaves slide,
truth elides, o shadow, o mother
burning your own effigy
swarming into fire
sucked deep into a wax under-
world where finally you are mine.

The Death Verses

To gallop into the void
on their wooden upside-down horses,
the Masters set down
their last verses:

1) Master Ta-kuan had no
energy to box anyone's
ears: *Yume*, he wrote—
Dream, and died.

2) When he wrapped
his legs full lotus, Master
Hofuku left ideation.

3) Chuang-tzu refused
the expensive funeral, but
not the carrion kites or
the crows. The cricket-moles
did not weep for his flesh.

4) Indescribable tenderness.

5) Bashō had no poem.
He had already died
to every moment, breathing
each brilliant fish to life.

Monet at Palazzo Contarini

What Venice is this, that in a rare gloom abraded by shadow who we have been echoes
as water does, being water. Innumerable mutations, vessels moving with dark oars—
transport of spices, then ashes, then seeds of the self. We glide past doorways,
past portals into the opulent immaterial. Under pediments, arches, bridges.
What slakes our thirst, what doesn't. Faces change as in a dream, as in my ducal procession—
all my doges—but that one: tried for treason, beheaded, his portrait blackened.
All my doges now lap the steps along the Grand Canal, along the seemly unseen. Under bridges,
I pass my lost body, return to night's singular entrance into some larger self.

O My Visitor: A Travelogue

1

Rome, day two, still jet-lagged—
I file toward the Colosseum, thronged by crowds.
By dusk, perch on a marble slab eating a pre-packaged salad
overlooking the Forum of Augustus, built to avenge the death of Caesar.
To the right, the excavated temple to Minerva, renamed the Forum of Nerva:
an assassination, intrigue, now just the jagged yellow teeth of spent bravado.
Trajan's emasculating column leers to my left, a raised narrative
like a texture I want to work under my tongue.

A sweating man hurls into view, asks a question in Italian. Looks
at my blank face, says *I am lost*. Adds*: so much better in Milan, no?
Signs tell you*. I cannot tell him the way.

After three minutes, he dissolves into a labial sunset.
Clouds form, preclude thought. Rome's pendulant horizon, mulled & exterior.

Don't yet know whether I will leave you. I travel alone.
But who can afford to dispense with other humans? Once
of course, we loved.
Two seagulls land, squawk for food—edge closer.
Eyes speculative as old men.

Beneath San Clemente Basilica, I regress into a 4th century cathedral.
Where once stood the impasto of madonna & child,
the wall fell to reveal the flat Byzantine faces of madonna & child.

Subterranean Rome where among five fir trees in a grove—another grove
entered by way of seven important eras.

2

Another grove entered by way of seven important eras.
Roam into the Roman Forum, unnoticed. College girls prop
their heads on empty pediments for pics in the ruined house
of the Vestal Virgins. Their year abroad— lithe with tans & corrected
teeth, oversharing their iphone images. One holds her screen up, says: *that
was the best day of my life*. They have i-phoned their yesterday back into existence.

Here the Vestal Virgins bent to keep the flame aglow—on punishment
of death. Black stones thicken in heat. My sole catches one & I stumble.
Where Caesar walked, signs say. But also: slaves.
Ovoid stones shimmer, oscillate.

Along the far wall, statues of the most famous Vestals, pocked
by weather. The first manikins: their faces wrecked. To consort
with a citizen was called *incestus* or treason against the city, the punishment
to be buried alive in an underground chamber. You could not spill the blood
of a virgin nor bury Romans within the city, but you could bear the Vestal Virgin
still alive on a bier through the streets, furnish a small meal, pull up the ladder & seal her in.

3

Pull up a ladder & seal her in. Brimmed by history: I look up into the Palazzo's
fresco. Float or fall into the angled & massacred heavens. Overtired from the heat,
drink a cappuccino from a machine & wire myself awake all night looking at another ceiling.

There are reasons for leaving. Selfish, hypocritical & an enabler. Who isn't, though? When
I finally fall asleep, you appear. Ask to build a table together. I'm sex-worn, constellated
by pinpoint stars. *No.* Your grown boy runs the car off road, flips another one,
grows immense like a Botero, writes a sequence called *The Junkie Poems*.
You laugh in the way you do. I'm living in your dream, not mine.

No, I said, *please no*. A young man stretches across three cushions of the settee looks up
at the *Allegory of Divine Providence and Barberini Power*. I throw out an arm to imitate &
he shifts his languid dominance, annoyed.

Overhead, the newly clothed Baroque. Golden bees, symbol for the Barberini clan, motor
in formation. I hear my mother crying in the stale back room of her chamber. Calling
my name until I become nameless. As children, we talk her down from death.

In the 70s, didn't we all recline in technicolor dark, watching B-movies, denying
that our mothers threatened suicide? At eleven, my tired sister said,
Don't go in there again. She's pretending.

Names burn through the Palazzo. Golden bees wind up Borromini's helicoidal staircase into the
cells of the honeycomb. Renaissance seekers learned bees obeyed the queen, not a king, so
noblemen destroyed the research. Their question: How could women have a soul?

Above, Minerva flies forward, armed with her mind to defeat the Giants, flesh
ruddy with shadows. My mother's dead now, but I go again & again to her hive. Below
Divine Providence, the simulated frame crumbles.

4

Below Divine Providence, the simulated frame crumbles. I take photographs
of people taking selfies in front of art figures like Raphael,
who painted himself in the crowd
of philosophers to stare back at the people taking selfies
in the arched rooms of the Vatican Museum.

Like Raphael, I see too much of myself. Legend has that he died of a fever at 37
after wild night-crushing sex with La Fornarina, the baker's daughter,
her eyes a delicious black.

Or maybe I don't see enough. Madonna wears her pale habit, windowless
crowns on saints, frescoes you could step into & out of. We peer into Christ's
ravaged soul or wearing his infant face, all forehead. His head inclines,
attuned to rumors of the absentee father.

There's *our father*, & my own, stroking his bald head—absent
for most of my childhood, or my daughter's father when she was just one day old.
Make her shut up. Each time he yells, I go to my knees, begging him to stop. *Our father,
who art in heaven.* How often do we fail to see patterns?

The further into Rome, the more I lose myself. Long
for those subterranean rooms: the reputed mithraeums. At the Barberini Museum,
try to buy a ticket to go underground, but the ticket-taker says *go to the National Museum*.
At the museum, a mystified ticket-taker says *No. No tickets here. Call this number.* The line
tuned to busy. A dead end. The next day, I run near the mithraeum at the Circus Maximus.

Below my feet, beneath Rome Opera's costume storeroom, once the former
Pantanella pastry shop, two centuries before Raphael's infant
Christ played with John the Baptist on the poor dirt of some far away Judea:
the myth of the Mithras plays out. He is a creature of light. Our origins
enacted by initiates. Some wear ravens or lions' heads, poised
at thresholds: the *transitus*. An engraving of Mithra's mantel held
by the Raven's beak. The scorpion latches to his ankle, waits as Mithra
kills the cosmic bull & creates the universe. The movement of his cloak gives rise
to the rotation of stars. My daughter's no longer one day old, but 19. The *transitus*: she's left
home to enter other rooms far away. I am invaded by absence, am an absence
walking below ground into seven interlocking rooms. Initiated into this moon,
mercury, venus, sun, mars, jupiter, and saturn.

5

Initiated into this moon, mercury, venus, sun, mars, jupiter and saturn, I am engulfed in your diorama. The endless room stretches: at the back you are chained to your computer, as in a cave, maneuvering shadows. Meanwhile the grown boy cannot restrain
his pit bull; pills litter every entrance. You stayed home rather than Rome.

On the plane, dozing after a glass of Delta wine, I saw death as a dissolution
into orbs of light. Atoms whirl into the DNA of everything. Existence unmasked—the raven, the lion—simulacra. As atom, I knew the art of knowing. Absorbed in pure
consciousness, basking with stars.

Then, passports, my suitcase thrown open on whirling carrels
animating our fluorescent exhaustion. End up near the Spanish Steps, in the room where John Keats died. Outside, tourists try to find shade, fill plastic water bottles from the spring water brimming Borromini's boat. Here, only one other acolyte and I pass
each other as if this were the church.

In the anteroom: his life mask of 1816. Amusement warms the stilled features—his mouth faintly quirks. Footsteps in, the sleigh bed where the white death overtook him, and there, poised in a lucite cube, the death mask: absent his force. A face: only temporary housing.

He had left this *vale of soul-making*, entered back into a universe without dimension. *Intelligences*, he wrote to his siblings George & Georgina, *are atoms of perception—they know and they see and they are pure...* The ceiling above: white beams and two dozen
finials the dying Keats stared into. Orbs and orbs: a trompe l'oeil of infinity. *...in short they are God—How then are Souls to be made? How then are these sparks which are God to have identity given them—*
so as ever to possess a bliss peculiar to each one's individual existence?
How, but by the medium of a world like this?

My life as one small bliss, one rotating orb: You: Aloft in an air balloon over Napa Valley, a day after our marriage, the high yellow grasses had the appearance of the rooted locks of being. In a dream a man walks across the aqueous planet into his temporary housing. A fox
runs across the pubis of earth.

6

Into his temporary housing, a fox runs across the pubis of earth. Around the Circus Maximus I run above the underground mithraeum, crunch white rocks under my feet like miniature skulls. A team of runners passes, calls out *Ciao*. All ebullient in the fresh
summer air. *Ciao... Ciao!*

That call trails, buoyant with vibrations. In every sound house the silences. I run across
the death of my mother, my father, their skulls & death itself: the violent burn
of their bones. My mother's bones a gray rubble in a plastic bag that my sister & I held
with wonder. My father's reclined in the coffin of this life's underground chamber.

When I call home, you are perfunctory, routine. We do not talk of your grown boy,
my daughter, or why I have come here. In the afternoon, I take a train to Assisi. Trains
clatter the other way, going to Rome. Windows frame the dissolution of faces, crowd
the *transitus*. In Assisi's upper chapel, a visual fable to detail St. Francis's life
in twenty-eight scenes. Giotto created the effect of peering into a series
of small rooms. In one: God's hand poised mid-panel as if tearing through
dimension's indigo fabric.

To separate: to cleave. The drapery on Giotto's figures almost metallic, the colors
nearly transparent, and yet, unlike Ciambue's oxidized by time, olive oil
has preserved them: a brilliance I fall into.

 For the night, an airless room in the basement under one of Assisi's many bakeries. Monks
wear earbuds, walk casually in Nikes. That night, Giotto's blue opens
the cavity in my dream. Inside, you swallow me. Inside, you are the scorpion
at the door. I waken with a sudden sting, long to feel the sacral earth embodied : apart.

7

I long to feel the sacral earth embodied, a part. Back in Rome & down Via de Corso,
shops emit privilege.

Against the wall next to Prada, a Roma supplicates her full body forward for money. Her coin
cup shakes, clutched between dirty time-worn hands. Three manikins shadow her in the Prada
window. Holding leather bags, glyphs incline, sexy-recumbent.

I want to beg like she does, o my visitor, to be ground under foot. Could lose myself, forget to
call you, forget to eat, to sleep. Is this not just a lavish sensorium
to open my bones into orbs? When the Roma rises next to me, one eye
missing, do I dream?

At Villa Borghese, Bernini's white marbles: seized silent in their mythic involutions. Pluto
clutches Persephone, his fingers press into her thigh's stilled milk. Cerberus: his three-headed
salivation. At Apollo and Daphne, I see our dissolution. You pace
to grab hold, a hand wraps my hip, grasps bark's sudden enclosure. Orbed,
the helicoidal aromas of these trees.

Leaves oranged, singed, and burned. Do I run from love or into?
Or is it the *transitus*: my leaves pump their seduction, cast off
what was never mine: a junkie forgetful indolence, a desire
to seal me in. Foot finds root, fuses to earth's atoms. Glance across this earth
but once. Something pursues & my arms
break into a thousand branches.

One, Another

When I hear my killer, I'm flat on my back
dreaming of a man I want to love despite
his face, half-burned. My spine contracts.
The ancients retreat, pool on furred surfaces. If
there's a personal self and the universal, I want
to live closer to the galaxy. My killer's majestic,
90 feet high, collecting years close under ridged
skin. My killer, ungendered, roots into the infinite,
touches the knuckles of other trees for miles. My killer
doesn't know me, just as my rapist didn't nor the one
I married. A foot pauses on the step—and we both
listen. I thought we had nothing in common,
ends up, we do. When I open the door, all the fine bones
splinter into music. When I open the door, I fly
through my killer's forehead into my own.

Snake Notice

Collecting zeroes . *narrow fellows* . Robert Mitchum cleft-chinned . bone-chilling bad boys . factual thump of your hand against my _____ . you light a cigarette . play an orange-inflected Fender Strat . zero in on Robert Plant's *Stairway to Heaven*: each hair backlit . fusing . infusing . bulbs urge underground . drunk, you drive the rust-infested Datsun in the snow . pawn your Strat . one year later lost on intestinal black roads . foothills near Tucson . tulips send up tough tongues of green . you seethe at me amid that beauty : those stars . those stars . Roger Daltrey's wiry tantric dance . you lose another job . we sit drinking margaritas for hours . throw us out for fighting . you yell back, stroke your mustache . speed out . find your dog tags from Vietnam so that part is true . love . hate tattooed on Mitchum's fingers . lacing . unlacing . blooms like crushed . we part like cyclones . decades later : internet mug shot . scarred shaven upper lip . *friendly fire* you'd said . Roger Daltrey's wizened jaunt as leprechaun . remember the factual thump of your hand against my forehead . those stars . zonked electric Robert Plant . you sat locked in that rust-bellied Datsun . held the syringe up at the window . *please stop* . Now your obit snakes in my face . absent the details . your mother's name tells me it's you . sang an electric *Good Night Irene* in that heat-slicked bar where you turned up . back-lit : your sex . heat that carbonite Mitchum . saying *please stop* . you thump down hard . to my knees . drunk mug shot . spent vet obit . Look how we pass each other on a footbridge over Tucson . as if we hadn't . that once *zero* . those stars
. *wrinkled* . *and was gone*

Honeymoon

On the trail, fox bones mistaken for tinder . bones through which I enter the inert long ago . solitary & briny as the disarticulated sex in that far away Mykonos . rooftops ridge the seaside like knobs on a spine . before we had gone there : did I really know you ? your face murky, unclear . further uphill possum bones : a tail like pink eraser heads steered by a thin trace of carrion beetles . time-lapsed in the shifting late August grass . what can I say about the big picture ? a hollow distance opened between us . my memory of the particulars smells like bad patchouli . once we got to Santorini you were dissatisfied . wondered aloud if we'd made a mistake . underground in the ruins of Akrotiri, we saw the first aqueducts . some night terror throttled through my body . left me off at the ground floor . your back solid . turned away . tourists thronged the volcanic ash beaches mostly nude . a portly German went crustacean-pink . read a book standing up . his small member shaded by his belly . he aimed himself . shadow lengthening . lapping the edges of our betrothal . I crossed my arms over my breasts in the photograph you took : a Cycladic figurine . feeling fat though I was small . going smaller . remember all the bodies I have occupied ? under leaves . bird bones as if immolated . in a past life regression. I'm a citizen of Akrotiri . stand phallus-proud on shore . fill the stone house of my marriage with the kind of mind-fuck you did for our next ten years . in Paros you walk off angry . leave me for three days alone . did I long for you ? no . I hiked the white-ribbed landscape in wonder . discovered the gold-pressed minotaur . knelt to roadside shrines . I stop now on the trail . bend to look at these small theaters . the body's diorama: alienating & plush . we said we loved each other once . became strangers again

A Sonic Crown of Bees

When we were in the story, moss, like feathers
blessed our feet where we walked. When we
were in the story, I wore your jockey shorts
and nothing else. The a-words came down like rain
that we licked, over-licked: a*mbivalence, ant, Apollo, arch,
& ask*. Your words told me I was beautiful, horny, smart and
sweet. Noon & still we stayed in the cove licking,
over-licking. Sun bedraggled the moss, everything plain—
then the bees' overture. When we look back on the story,
we may watch it change—the *a*'s were unspoken, I
was horny, but not sweet enough. The bees had pearled
into death. The cove collects moss, co-exists with the story—
sometimes inhabited by humans, sometimes storyless,
accruing a's: *acid, allegory, apocalypse, amens.*

Grammar

You said bears walk in the wealthy hamlet of Aspen . don't we say *lumber* when it comes to bears ? the verb itself the journey we imagine the bear encounters in the topographical skull of its bigger mind .   a man sits on his back deck to cough up his smoker's phlegm near dawn . a wracking sound shudders across backyards . obscures the sonorous buzzing I've grown accustomed to : insects sheathe the morning in their bugginess . like so many jewels birds will join in . start with a few calls : a warble then a chirrup enlarges to a syntax supple with sound . I will not call them *plaintive* or *enchanted* . no ideas to attach them to . though our mouths may turn lonely in the flush morning of our greed .   I rose at midnight from the bed where we once *lay* . or is it *laid* ? my grammar sticky . our lies having reclined all around us . through the open door a fox without an adjective appeared one night .   my same wildness staring back .   in the end you did not *lumber* away . in the creaturely grammar of this world : a fox is *fleet* footed . wears a *silvered* pelt . your light feet fox-turning you sheer as dream .   everything about us is instantaneous .   we are immense .   without cause & often ineffectual . the   hide of who we   are disappearing .   only ourselves   .   in the skin of the beloved

The Fantasists of the Earth

enter through the pores in your body—
looking, as you do, at the sacred: materials
of the past, playthings of the future.
They create terrains: tiered
rice paddies in China, towering cliffs
in Ethiopia. In Bolivia, sand reddens
into a branching tree of life.
They don't know you when you look at them,
or do they? They touch the objects
you touch, hold the scents of those
you once loved. Under balconies,
they roam the carbon streets
uttering curses, hunched into their mania,
brow-first. One carries his many-
sheaved books; another constructs
the human face from nothing, hammers
the graven images of your eyes. They crystallize only
when you choose to see. You walk among
fantasists, enter an untimed time, released
from the arbitrary cells you were born into.
The fantasists are you, in you, infuse
the riddle of every self-same tree.
We enter each other's physics—
beheld / beholding.

Mourning Dove

Too heavy for the feeder,
it pecks at the squirrel's
spent seeds.

No, this isn't
a nature poem, or
how the bird's

call reminds me
of my Grandma Doe's
home in Ohio.

If I were a certain
professor poet, I'd
recall that bar

in Philly and perch
on a memory like
I was told, waiting

for Beau or Buster
or Brad to grab
a beer and bawl—

But no, everything
you've been taught
about poetry

is false. Our mourning
is inglorious; our
constitutions weak.

Among the scabrous
weeds, the dove
has nothing to give me

nor represent, its
material shudder and
half-flight as

illusory as the grit
it eats to break
down seeds.

The Hallelujahs light-
splotched and shuttered
by the figments

of loss.

Jewelweed

Gibbous moon or no
my teeth grind
on the inevitable.
Beside me
you vibrate
in several dimensions
unbothered.

Sir Isaac Newton aged
into his character armor.
All the ways we go rigid
in the world.
By 1726, he appears corpulent
with science,
a method to unceasingly
nail the coffin
on wonder.

We went further
into the woods
leaving our selves
behind.
      Some
flowers throated.
Amid rain
we go translucent.

Creaturely

Easy to think substance will last forever.
The green-brown water I swim through
swims through me. The Muong family laughs
when a turtle swerves beyond
the buoy and away. Cool immediate
fingers—lake fronds anointing me—but to what?
I will never be one of the Muong family from
the inside. Dusk descends
as the teenage daughter turns in her neon
green t-shirt. We two, the last in the lake.
Her smile, velvet anemones, cloud windows,
vitreous minnows scatter at my feet. My whole life lived
in increments of three. Have we not
the muscle of god in us amid
these substances? Her sister on shore sings
words she learned at school, turns them
into a hummed lathe. I'm no longer afraid
of poverty as I should be, but only
through temporary reprieve. Do we all step out
of our angel bodies or do our angel bodies step into us?
Here in my thingy self, I watch the lake surface innocent
of people—creaturely though—sliding convex
through filaments of space where
I am the no-god drowning, where
what is human—once anointed—passes on.

Ghost Pipes

Each stem bears only one flower
Monotropa = Greek for one turn

.

Over 2,000 Instagram posts to
Monotropa Uniflora—
skeletal, turning their necks down

.

or away

.

from terror
Discovered broken-backed
but alive among corpses—
There's just the going through—the holocaust
survivor—once a dancer—says

.

A night of dreams, the word
elocutions repeated

.

I walk behind you into Smithgall
Woods/ among mountain laurel
cupped blooms flushing
not our skins
but the skin of our skins

.

a voice in the dream
interrogatory: *whom
did it change outside
the sphere of influence?*

.

It being the woods?
It being how we came here?
It being the risks we took?

.

Not fungus, not reliant on sun, not with color
nor love for it,
not undulant, nor weak

.

interior, reliant
on nearby mushrooms
and trees –

.

Forced to dance for her bread
she shared it with the other rubbed-
away girls—eyes moons of
suggestion

.

It = all that we've used up
housed & bending corpse
heads to the ground

.

each mouth's sensation sent
through nerve-like filaments
a radical mutualism

.

To stop was to be shot
on the Death March
Marthausen to Gunskinchen
35 miles—

.

when
her spine broke—
the girls carried her

.

by November, you were gone

.

What disappears that we didn't invoke
before?

Dendrochronology

She denudes as all trees do
whether of leaf, or by
decomposition. What's left
but her torso, bleached. She's
all clock now, bark
only the dropped skin where air once
touched her. My beautiful
figment—a dryad for dark
measures. After your massive fall,
how you shuddered
and throbbed in my blood.
As mistake, curse, or something
I could fix, rather than *writ
in water*; water you took
in beats from a conscious
tangled underwood. You:
mote, spoke, brought noon—
lost your storied canopy.
Your ruin, my waking. Both
of a mind to roam. Not
timepieces after all. What
decays? *By whom shall
the knower be known?*

Trees Flee
    after Rilke

Every year the fig tree grows more
grandiose— its clown hands
flapping with contentment –
its fruits so pendulous, a cardinal
merely strokes one like a nipple.
Late summer unfolds—the tree's
thirst: mine. As if we will always be
in this charged eros, this air.
I mash figs, turn them under
my spoon into ruby jam rife
with a million seeds— atoms vibrating
both complete and boundless. Because
the hurricane took down my oak, the fig's
canopy overtakes the laurel, as Apollo did,
swarming his god hands so near the nymph
she broke her arms into untold branches—
closed and otherless. Was it desire?
Or was it the spell we were under—
an endless pursuit, grasping at what
was never ours? What made us think
we couldn't kill a world?

Notes

The epigraph is from *Rilke's Book of Hours*, I,3, translated by Anita Barrows & Joanna Macy—

"The Ledgers" borrows lines from Wallace Stevens's "The Dove in the Belly"—

"Bayou Ghost Trees" makes use of Wikipedia entries on Jean LaFitte as well as facts on environmental damage to the Barataria region of Louisiana—

"Death-Moth" owes its title to John Keats—as well as a few lines from his work—

Quotes in "Footnoting Luce" are from Irigaray's *This Sex Which Is Not One*—

"Jekyll" has its origin in the history of Jekyll Island, a barrier island off the coast of Georgia—winter home for the oligarchs of the early twentieth century—

"The Omitted Center" is rooted in Jay Leyda's term for the missing piece that may explain Emily Dickinson's work. *"it's late Miss Dickinson"*: her father frequently entreated her to go to sleep rather than to stay up writing. Also used: Dickinson lines & ways of describing trauma: "numb circuit" and "blank-to-blank"—

"Calaveras Big Tree" stems from the 19th century exhibition trees: several giant sequoias, many measuring over 24 feet in diameter, were harvested then reassembled for display at world's fairs and international expositions. These spectacles, before photography, were sometimes seen as hoaxes; their unfortunate plunder, however, and thankfully, led to conservation efforts and protection areas in state parks—

"The Death Verses" includes incidents described in Yoel Hoffman's book, *Japanese Death Poems Written by Zen Monks and Haiku Poets on the Verge of Death*—

In "O My Visitor…" lines from Keats are from a letter to his siblings, dated April 21, 1819. Information on Mithraism as well as all references to underground tourist sites are from *Subterranean Rome*, by Ivana Della Portella—

"Snake Notice" plays with phrases from Dickinson's poem 1096 (Franklin edition) that begins "A narrow fellow in the grass" –

"Jewelweed" makes use of ideas about Isaac Newton in Morris Berman's *The Reenchantment of the World*—

"Dendrochronology" nods to Keats's "writ in water" and ends with a line from *The Upanishads*—

Acknowledgments

Birdcoat Quarterly: "O My Visitor: A Travelogue"
Birmingham Poetry Review: "Calaveras Big Trees" and "The Ledgers"
Bluestem: "Snake Notice"
Canopic Jar: "Fireflied"
Counterclock Journal: "Hover" and "The Death Verses"
Community of Writers Review: Bayou Ghost Trees"
Denver Quarterly: "Manhattan" and "Death-Moth"
Glass: A Journal of Poetry: "Cabinet of Obsessions"
Green Mountains Review: "Uprooted"
Hotel Amerika: "Those Ghost Selves"
Juked: "Footnoting Luce"
Menacing Hedge: "The Omitted Center"
The Mom Egg Review: "Birthday Month"
Phi Kappa Phi Forum: "Jewelweed"
Pithead Chapel: "Annihilation," "Grammar," and "Honeymoon"
Pleiades: "One, Another"
Quaint Magazine: "The Moveable Charolais"
Rabbit Catastrophe Review: "Baby Teeth"
Ruminate: "The Dash"
Soundings East: "The Great Composers" as "The Lives of the Great Composers," and "Jekyll," as "A Sensuous Proposal"
Stirring: "Communion," "Disaster Relief," "Unsalvageable + Scented," and "Mourning Dove"
storySouth: "Enter at Castello di Vezio"
Tinderbox Poetry Journal: "A Sonic Crown of Bees" and "Ghost Pipes"
Two Hawks Quarterly: "Trees Flee"
Waterstone Review: "Red Oak, Black Oak"

Thanks go to the amazing individuals in two writing groups where some of these poems received assistance: The Good Bones group—Jo Brachman, Jen Colatosti, and Lisa Allen plus George's pre- and post Covid group—Beth Gylys, Jennifer Wheelock, Cathy Carlisi, Ashley Grice, and Michael Walls. My thanks also go to Claire Bateman, Jade Rivers, and Sandy Meek for your encouragement and insights. As well, my thanks to the many giving people in my life who helped me during my time as a climate change refugee—you helped me on my feet again and you are in my heart. Gratitude to Hambidge Center for the Creative Arts and Sciences and its spacious abiding—

ALSO BY AMY PENCE

*Your Posthumous Dress: Remnants
from the Alexander McQueen Collection*

[It] Incandescent

Armor, Amour

The Decadent Lovely

Skin's Dark Night

ABOUT THE AUTHOR

Amy Pence authored the poetry collections *The Decadent Lovely* (Main Street Rag, 2010), *Armor, Amour* (Ninebark Press, 2012) as well as the chapbooks *Skin's Dark Night* (2River Press, 2003) and *Your Posthumous Dress: Remnants from the Alexander McQueen Collection* (dancing girl press, 2019). Her hybrid book, *[It] Incandescent* (Ninebark, 2018)— with Emily Dickinson at its speculative center—won the Eyelands International Poetry Award in Greece. She's also published short fiction, interviews, and essays in a variety of journals and magazines, including *WHR, WSQ, The Writer's Chronicle,* and *Poets & Writers*. Red Hen Press will publish her debut novel, *Yellow*, in 2026. She taught composition and creative writing classes for many years, including poetry writing at Emory, tutored high-schoolers at Pace Academy, and continues as a part-time tutor in Atlanta.

www.ingramcontent.com/pod-product-compliance
Lightning Source LLC
Chambersburg PA
CBHW040009080526
44586CB00028B/2944